SMART

storage solutions

CountryLiving

Creative Closets, Stylish Shelves & More

Valerie Rains

HEARST BOOKS

New York

HEARST BOOKS
New York

An Imprint of Sterling Publishing
387 Park Avenue South
New York, NY 10016

ISBN 978-1-61837-144-7

Distributed in Canada by Sterling Publishing
c/o Canadian Manda Group, 165 Dufferin Street
Toronto, Ontario, Canada M6K 3H6

Distributed in the United Kingdom by GMC Distribution Services
Castle Place, 166 High Street, Lewes, East Sussex, England BN7 1XU
Distributed in Australia by Capricorn Link (Australia) Pty. Ltd.
P.O. Box 704, Windsor, NSW 2756, Australia

For information about custom editions, special sales, and premium and corporate purchases, please contact Sterling Special Sales at 800-805-5489 or specialsales@sterlingpublishing.com.

Manufactured in China

2 4 6 8 10 9 7 5 3 1

www.sterlingpublishing.com

Foreword

Personality. Character. Style. The guiding lights we rely on when we decorate our homes have a way of flickering out when the time comes to organize our closets, stow off-season goods for the year, or bring order to an overflowing pantry. (After all, when did a clear plastic tub ever set someone's heart aglow?) But it doesn't have to be that way. Storage can be soulful. Your approach to living with the objects you love (or at least can't get by without) can say as much about your tastes as the artwork you hang on the wall. Heck, sometimes a treasured (but tricky-to-store) collection of weathered watering cans (p. 150) or vintage rolling pins (p. 86) can even *become* the artwork on your wall.

In this book, we'll go room by room, teasing out unexpected (but wholly effective) ways to contain clutter and create calm without losing an ounce of originality. The ideas all come from homes we've featured in the magazine, which means that people like you (and us!)—with their own antiques obsessions, sentimental attachments, and piled-high potting sheds—have already done the hard work of figuring out how to display prized possessions without feeling suffocated by them (it's all about editing), how to put trusty standbys to new use (see the genius kitchen command station made out of an old armoire) and how to harness the transformative power of a coat of paint. The best examples exhibit a magician's sleight of hand—managing to look like they have absolutely nothing to hide while still delivering delightful surprises around every corner.

Ready to add to your own bag of storage and organizing tricks? Turn the page. We're thrilled to reveal our secrets.

< Got baggage? An immoderate affection for vintage suitcases becomes an asset when your favorite specimens are stacked to the ceiling and filled with things you only need access to once in a while (beach towels and sun hats, say).

Welcoming Living Rooms

In the living room, as in life, balance is everything. Fill the room with too many trinkets, and you risk crowding your guests beyond the point of comfort (and perhaps leaving them with nowhere to set a drink). Pare down too much, on the other hand, and you lose that richness of detail that makes your home unique.

In this chapter, we've rounded up dozens of ways to combat clutter while preserving coziness—some of which don't cost a dime. First, hunt for double-duty furniture, such as a roomy vintage trunk that provides storage while also standing. Then, take time to consider overlooked corners: Could that one fit an L-shaped banquette with built-in drawers? And don't hesitate to tweak what you already have to better suit your needs. A few salvaged cabinet doors added to a standard bookcase let you decide what to enclose and what to expose.

Once you've carved out some hardworking hiding spaces, you can focus on the fun part—creating harmonious displays of the items you want to flaunt. We've included inspiration for that, too—from museum-worthy arrangements of antiques to novel ideas for storing books.

< This room's monochromatic palette keeps the wall-
spanning array of whitewave from verging into chaos,
as do the simple upholstered chairs and slipcovered
ottoman. An ivory trunk conceals more prosaic pieces.

Practice Creative Adaptation

The quickest way to add character to a living room? Employ ordinary objects in inventive ways. It instantly creates areas of wonder and interest (and will likely inspire a few "Why didn't I think of that?" musings when guests swing by). Whether that means rejiggering a store-bought item for greater usefulness or entirely reimagining a piece of furniture's purpose, there's no need to settle for off-the-rack storage solutions.

When recast as a magazine rack, a simple wooden ladder gives new life to a little-used corner, while nearby, an affordable armoire outfitted with a pair of mirrors elegantly hides a television set and other electronics. Currently a receptacle for a jumble of glass fishing floats, this $3 flea-market crate could easily take on more practical duties—such as holding cozy throws or reading materials. And that Ikea ottoman? It's hollow inside for even more secret storage.

bright idea!
Use the cabinet's bottom drawers for DVDs and compact discs.

A trio of repurposed cabinet doors (added to this bookcase after the fact) balances out the wide, unbroken upper shelves and creates a low-profile hiding place for anything not quite worthy of the spotlight.

The shallow drawers of an antique flat file are just the right size for containing coasters, remote controls, or even taper candles and tea lights. Bulkier stuff (say, board games or dog toys) can reside inside an old wood tool chest that doubles as a low side table.

Bibliophiles, take note: This vintage card catalog could hold its own as a merely decorative item, but its dozens of compartments are capable of so much more. Designate one row for basic tools (a hammer and nails, screwdrivers, picture-hanging kits); one for electronic accessories (phone and camera chargers and cables); and one for spare keys. (You can always add labels if you're afraid you'll forget what's where.)

A secondhand mantel (scored for about 100 bucks on eBay) not only bestows architectural depth on a plain, boxy room, it also acts as an attractive shelf for books or family photos, while subtly evoking the warmth of a fireplace.

bright idea!
Facing books spines in, pages out, makes for a striking—and novel—display.

One Essential Trick:
Try a Storage Table

The iterations are endless, but the impact is always the same: Opting for a side table, coffee table, or end table with built-in storage (even if that "table" used to be a barrel, a bucket, or a trunk) instantly adds utility to a room—without claiming any extra square footage.

In basic plywood, this crate-like coffee table loosens up the antique seriousness of its ornate surroundings—and holds loads. And thanks to the low material costs, having one custom made is less expensive than buying even a much-smaller model in a typical furniture store.

A faded blue coffee bean bucket perks up a fireside seating area while offering covert storage beneath its lid. One bright idea for what to stash inside: Flashlights, candles, and batteries for a dark and stormy night.

Large pieces of masculine leatherbound luggage can harbor oversized items (think sleeping bags, guest pillows, or seasonal centerpieces).

ANATOMY OF AN ORGANIZED LIVING ROOM

Bursting with tricks for taming the clutter of daily life, this blue and white beauty is all about choosing what to highlight and what to hide.

1. A clever cabinet built into a recess above the nonworking fireplace conceals a television set.

2. The coffee table, actually a vintage wicker trunk, makes short-notice stow-away jobs a total breeze.

3. Openwork rattan chairs offer an airy counterpart to the solid sofa and sizeable trunk.

4. Enlivened with blue paint, the built-in bookcases call attention to the dynamic arrangements of objects, while matching white baskets house smaller odds and ends.

5. A generous tray atop the trunk brings together books, a bowl, and a bouquet to make a single, cohesive style statement.

6. A woven basket gives easy access to blankets and throws.

Put Prized Possessions in Their Place

The difference between an impressive collection with mass appeal and, well, a mess? Identifying ways to bring harmony to the whole while letting individual pieces sing—whether everything's out in the open, under glass, or behind closed drawers. When the objects in question differ in color, shape, or size, keep the display simple and streamlined, forgoing any fussy extras that might make it feel old-fashioned. With a monochrome collection, on the other hand, mix in a few wild-card components that don't fit the theme to ward off monotony. (Just keep them muted, so they don't compete for attention.)

Built-in shelves that were too short for storing books have been repurposed to showcase a trove of vintage toolboxes, jewelry boxes, and file boxes in a range of earthy hues. And with the help of a set of handmade library stairs, even the boxes on the highest shelves can be used as storage devices in their own right.

When displaying several collections in one go, positioning the least-functional objects in the hardest-to-reach place can be a smart move. Here, elevating a row of vintage fire extinguishers made room for more-useful industrial finds, such as books, buckets, and small chests, nearer to eye level.

A grouping of birds' nests that otherwise would have gobbled up shelf space (not to mention gathering dust) gets the museum treatment in a glass-topped curio table with a bonus, now-you-see-it, now-you-don't drawer.

Beautify Your Bookcases

If you have 50 books or 5,000, it's worth giving your shelves some love. Here are four foolproof facelifts to try, whether you're a stickler for Dewey-Decimal-style systems or just want things to look pretty.

Present a unified front, covering some spines in matching paper (or flipping books on their sides) to effect the look. Intersperse with like-colored objects and artwork to add texture and dimension.

bright idea!
Stacked books make great risers for small sculptural items, providing the height needed to fill up a tall shelf.

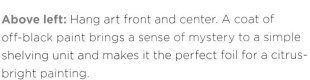

Above left: Hang art front and center. A coat of off-black paint brings a sense of mystery to a simple shelving unit and makes it the perfect foil for a citrus-bright painting.

Above right: Group by hue, alternating the orientation of the stacks and mixing in shapely extras to break up the boxiness.

Left: Go over the top, stacking volumes all the way to the ceiling (and turning the bookcase's color up to 11).

Or Store Books in Offbeat Spots

Great literature can take you places you never imagined. Why not return the favor? Consider it a plot twist for your personal library and for your decor.

Humble periodicals go high-concept on a long, lofty shelf with a contrasting wall for a backdrop. Old National Geographics created the sunny stripe here, but other spines make bold statements, too.

A glossy, Chinese-red door with a built-in bookcase? As thrilling as a secret passageway, but without the how-the-heck-do-you-open-it intrigue.

From liability to library: Repurpose a nonworking fireplace for free-form book storage. The quincy arrangement might even kindle renewed interest in some long-forgotten titles.

Don't Be Afraid to Mix Things Up

Sticking to a single storage strategy (built-ins on every wall, an army of armoires) can end up feeling staid and stiff. But those same elements, when mixed up, recombined, and scattered around, breathe life and style into a room. You don't have to go totally nuts—a few unexpected choices here and there can make all the difference.

This lake house's happy hodgepodge of built-in cubbies and freestanding lockers proves the appeal of a loose, laid-back approach to organizing. The owners' motto? Store here, there, and everywhere. They even capitalized on the niches over the windows, using them as shadowboxes for nature-inspired knickknacks.

Above: Let utility and décor rub shoulders. Juxtaposing functional items (folded Pendleton blankets, piles of vintage hardcover books) with ornamental ones (wood corner blocks treated as sculpture) invites interaction.

Left: Three steps to a tidy tabletop: Grab a bowl from the kitchen to display photos and postcards. Stack books to form pedestals for eye-catching keepsakes. And call upon a shallow planter to double as a snappy remote control caddy. Voila—order that's made to order (assembled with objects you already own).

Make Every Corner Count

Chances are, there's a least one solid storage opportunity right beneath your nose, just waiting to be noticed. Look high and low, over, under, inside, around, and through. (Channel Dr. Seuss if it helps.) Examine each hollow, hallway, eave, ledge, and landing. Having trouble? Invite a friend over to help identify underutilized space—sometimes it takes a fresh pair of eyes to uncover it.

This area by the stairs could have easily been written off as a mere way station for coats and umbrellas. Instead, an L-shaped daybed with built-in drawers offers an inviting nook for napping, a casual space for conversation, and oodles of useful storage.

Left: Positioning this pile of reading materials underneath a side table allows a perky potted topiary to claim its day in the sun. A stable stack of large-format tomes can even sub in for a side table if you'd like.

Below: Here, a row of cubbies under the window seat have been turned over to easy-to-reach but out-of-the-way fire-wood storage. (The act of removing the cabinet's doors revealed their potential in a flash.)

Thanks to its ample lower shelf, this reclaimed-elm coffee table boasts double the surface area of a standard version, so reading materials can be out when you want them to be and (almost) invisible when you don't.

HOMEWORK

Carve out a covert remote control holder inside a book.

Unlike *Downton Abbey,* your clunky clicker isn't exactly a must-see. So why not stash the eyesore in a book?

1. Choose a book that's at least two inches longer and ¼ inch deeper than your remote control (and not ripe for a repeat reading).

2. Open the book's back cover. Using a foam brush, coat the inside cover and facing page with school glue. Close the book and press down firmly for 10 seconds.

3. Open the book's front cover. Coat the entire stack of pages—all three exposed sides—with school glue, taking care not to get any on the topmost page. Let dry for one hour; repeat. Close the book, weight it with a second book, and let dry overnight.

4. Open the front cover, center your remote on the first page, and trace around it with a pencil, adding ¼ inch all the way around. Set the remote aside. With an X-Acto knife, cut along the marked line, removing two to three pages at a time. Continue until your remote fits completely inside.

5. Cut a piece of ribbon that's half the length of your book plus five inches. Trim one end into a fork; dot hot glue on the opposite end, and affix it in the bottom-center of the hollowed-out area. The "bookmark" will lift out your neatly disguised device.

Serene Bedrooms

Even the fluffiest pillows and downiest duvet can't eliminate the unsettling effects of a messy bedroom. After all, if the last thing you see before turning out the light is a chaotic vanity strewn with jewelry, mismatched socks dangling from dresser drawers, and towering stacks of half-read books that threaten to topple at any second, how are you supposed to summon sweet dreams? Good news: Creating the kind of soothing, streamlined haven that lets you rest easy every night and awaken each morning ready to face the day is simpler than you may have imagined. In this chapter, we delve into ideas for uncovering valuable storage opportunities (hint: look under the bed), adapting (and adding to) closet space to accommodate your wardrobe, and cultivating serenity through the smart use of color. And while revamping the boudoir won't necessarily rid you of all your worries overnight, it's certain to brighten your outlook on a daily basis.

< On either side of Anthropologie's wrought-iron bed frame, mirrored nightstands tuck away novels, night creams, and other bedtime must-haves while subtly bouncing light around the room. The glam little numbers provide the perfect counterpoint to the rustic basket that holds spare blankets at the foot of the bed.

Discover the Beauty of Blending In

There's a reason this is a go-to decorator's trick: Painting all the walls (and even some of the larger furnishings) in a single muted shade not only conjures a calm vibe—it also creates the illusion of more space. And it may even inspire you to tidy up more often, so great is the satisfaction of returning the monochromatic room to order.

Here's an impressive vanishing act: A few coats of dusky purple paint deftly disguise this bedroom's built-in cabinets—even though they cover the entire floor-to-ceiling expanse. Super-long drapes in the same hue contribute to the effect, while layering on depth and texture.

Awash in white and decked out with rough-hewn woods, this cloudlike space is downright transcendent. Its well-chosen storage pieces practically disappear into the woodwork— and even the distressed trunk finds convenient camouflage in the reclaimed-fir floorboards.

Don't Be Afraid to Hide Under the Bed

The domain of dust bunnies alone? Hardly. This is prime real estate—particularly in spaces like kids' rooms and guest rooms that tend to have little of it to begin with. Relocating some quotidian essentials to this low-profile spot can really pay off.

A lofted sleeping nook takes the strategy to a whole other level, with cubbies for magazines, books, and spare sheets. (And what young person doesn't relish the chance to clamber up a ladder before lights-out?)

Built-in drawers beneath a guest room daybed serve as a convenient supply station for extra towels, toiletries, and other make-them-feel-at-home amenities (such as an alarm clock, eye mask, and a few classic paperbacks).

No brightly colored plastic toy chests here! Instead, a mismatched suite of vintage luggage whisks away figurines and games and slides right beneath the iron bed. The idea travels well, too—linens, out-of-season clothing, and photo albums could all get a similar first-class upgrade.

Find New Purpose for Old Furnishings

Bringing in furniture and accent pieces from other areas of the house can add some welcome diversity to the standard bedroom set—and gives you even more places to stash your stuff. The only limit is your imagination.

Industrial canvas hampers corral pillows and blankets (and high-ranking stuffed animals) for the little campers who'll bed down on these antique wood military cots.

It's a study in efficiency: A vintage school desk earns extra style credit while offering twice the surface area of a traditional nightstand. Suspending a lamp from the ceiling liberates even more room for reading materials.

Spindly side tables work fine for some folks, but a low-rise dresser (one that's similar in height to the bed) can do so much more with a similar footprint. Your favorite pajamas will always be within arm's reach.

bright idea!:
Transform a dresser with chic wallpaper instead of paint or stain.

One Essential Trick:
Pack a Linens Trunk

Free up some real estate in the hall closet and keep your most cherished comforters and coverlets in the room where you'll actually use them. A vintage travel trunk or storage chest does the job with style.

Nestled in the nonworking fireplace, this weather-beaten chest contains other ways to keep warm: stacks of woolen blankets and woven throws.

Folk art painting enlivens this trusty number, scored at a local antiques shop.

Why settle for a narrow bench when you can have a sturdy perch *and* storage? An old steamer trunk really goes the distance.

ANATOMY OF AN ORGANIZED BEDROOM

This peaked-roof room proves that peaceful (and practical) bedrooms come in all shapes and sizes.

1. The low, wide sewing cabinet that stands in for a headboard seems tailor-made for the unique room shape: It's loaded with drawers for discreet storage but doesn't overwhelm the limited visual space.

2. Instead of dismissing the sloped sides of the room as unusable, deep matching closets maximize the square footage and lend symmetry.

3. Adding the closets also created a reading nook just large enough for a pair of slim, streamlined chairs and a shared side table.

4. Ultra thin articulated sconces shed light on the sitting area and couldn't be less obtrusive. Even the pale shades seem to disappear.

5. A narrow ledge beneath the windows shows off a collection of mercury-glass bottles (which also moonlight as vases).

6. Small rugs on either side of the bed work with the scale of the room while still providing a soft place to land.

Redesign (and Redefine) the Closet

Let's be honest. Who doesn't wish for more space for your clothes (and shoes, and bags) now and then? But you don't have to knock down a wall to expand your wardrobe-wrangling options. If you can hang a curtain, mount a closet bar, or climb a ladder, a grander garment-storage system can be yours.

Even the awkward space under an eave can host a half-height bar for shirts and jackets, with just enough room for a row of shoes below. A free-standing cabinet painted to match the walls holds folded items.

Equipped with a rolling library ladder (fashioned from a wooden street find and a hardware kit), a pair of overhead cubbies can serve as a mini-attic for out-of-season outfits, outerwear, and shoes.

A guest room that only gets used a few times a year is a major missed opportunity. Reimagined as a walk-in closet, with opulent extras like a gold-trimmed vanity, pink-denim ottoman, and glinting, crystal-draped chandelier, it becomes a year-round indulgence (that's also a better use of the space). A combo of wall-mounted and rolling closet bars do the heavy lifting, and the wheeled ones can be relocated when visitors do come to stay.

bright idea!
Crates on the lower shelves of the rolling racks can collect handbags and hats.

Opposite: These masculine metal bins could be receptacles for almost anything, including undergarments, gym clothes, and winter gear. Set inside an open console, they consume less visual space than solid furniture would, and can easily be removed for reloading.

Above: Time for a curtain call! The no-carpentry closet (simply a section of wall cordoned off with draperies) takes on quiet glamour when gussied up with a matching valance.

Right: All you need to turn any corner into a closet worth showing off: a long, high shelf for totes, tins, and odds and ends; a sturdy bar; and a few breathable bins to keep shoes together. The only rule? Before you bare, you must pare. (Just picture the same setup with thrice as many hangers angling for space.)

Left: A vanity-top vignette of milkglass vessels (for holding bangles and cuffs) and a DIY vertical organizer (for hanging danglers) frees up surfaces and turns your accessories obsession into a decorative asset. To make the display, simply cover particleboard in gift wrap, then pop it into an ornate frame.

Below: One smart idea that's even more stylish than the sum of its parts: Stash delicate pendants and earring pairs in individual numbered containers to ensure that singles never go astray and chains never get tangled. Assign baubles to boxes in order or preference, day of the week, or the number of compliments you get when you wear them.

Sometimes, flaunting your finery just makes sense. This collection of chapeaux reads as whimsical artwork when hung on a wall (instead of clogging up the closet). Below, pretty patterned scarves spill out of a wicker basket atop the dresser.

The trendiest topper gets classical appeal when perched atop a plaster bust— and you'll never lose your head searching for it in a rush. The same idea works for bulky, hard-to-store necklaces or a beloved silk scarf.

Embellish a by-the-book dresser with removeable decals and snazzy drawer pulls.

A hand-me-down, 1980s relic (complete with wood-veneer drawer fronts) started a whole new chapter courtesy of a few coats of paint and a set of alphabet decals. Here's how to copy the A-plus look:

1. Start by removing the old hardware and gently sanding the surface of the drawer fronts.

2. Apply a layer of spray-on primer and let dry for two hours.

3. Next, go over everything with two coats of white water-based latex interior paint (we chose a semi-gloss finish). Use a roller for the first layer for quick coverage and a paintbrush for the second to create a slightly textured effect.

4. After the paint dries (you may want to wait a few full days), start playing around with the decal placement. While you experiment, use painter's tape to hold them temporarily in place.

5. When you've settled on a design, adhere the decals to the dresser using a burnishing tool (a credit card works in a pinch).

6. Screw in the new hardware and slice the stickers along drawer edges with a craft knife.

Inviting Dining Rooms

Every hostess worth her salt knows that unforgettable dinner parties—to say nothing of stylish celebration brunches and joyful cocktail affairs—aren't just a matter of what you serve. There's also a scene to be set, as well as a table. This is your chance to bring your most cherished plates out to play—and to display them, too. (That eclectic assortment of whiteware can transform into breathtaking wall art with a few savvy moves.) And thinking about the flow of the room—what you use when, and how often—can help you design a setup that truly serves your purposes, whether you thrive on formal gatherings or live for laid-back (or last-minute) shindigs. Want to encourage meals to happen at the dinner table every time? Keep utensils in a drawer built into the table, rather than in the kitchen (where they're more likely to be carried elsewhere). Wish you always had a soundtrack for memorable meals? Try stocking a bar station next to the stereo for a subtle reminder. And if you consistently find yourself drifting outside at the first sign of mild weather, fill a potting bench with entertaining supplies. You'll never have to scramble for the shatterproof dishes or hurricane lanterns again.

< In this elegantly spare space, an open, salvaged-elm shelving unit filled with glass vessels and stacks of cream-colored dishes amplifies the airy feeling. Wicker chairs subtly reference the California home's coastal location, while allowing light to filter through.

Celebrate Your Tastes

The things that most thrill you in life—whether that means literature, music, art pottery, or a really nice glass of Rioja—can provide the backdrop (and the inspiration) for endless dinner-table conversation when brought into the dining room and put on view. Lining the walls with books or wine bottles is also a great way to cozy up a banquet-size room that only hosts extra-large groups once in a blue moon.

Why waste precious basement space on boxes when you could have a divine subterranean dining room *and* a wine cellar? That's the idea behind this atmospheric cave accented with dramatic touches like the rust-colored chandelier and a bust of Bacchus. Stacked Belgian grape-gathering crates cradle the vintages and a massive gilded mirror maximizes the low light in a wholly romantic way.

bright idea!

The shelf above the doorway links a pair of bookcases in an archival arch.

This room's generous ceiling height and unobtrusive pocket doors allowed for the installation of built-in bookcases that hold the homeowner's stockpile of travel, gardening, and art books. Along with the Art Deco Chinese rugs and trove of English transferware, they speak volumes about their owners' interests.

Conceal and Reveal

A room with exclusivly closed-up storage can feel heavy, dark, foreboding—in short, the exact opposite of welcoming. But that doesn't mean you need to keep every last butter knife out on display. Splitting the difference—choosing wisely what to exhibit and what to hide away—yields a happy medium that effortlessly shifts from everyday utility to big-night elegance.

A stately hutch with some glass-front doors and some solid ones is like two pieces of furniture in one. Paired with an antique table, decorative wainscoting, and "wallpaper" made from faded book pages, it looks every bit the part of a well-preserved heirloom, rather than the discount-store steal it actually was.

Left: A combined kitchen and dining area that's open to the rest of the house calls for even more adroit storage solutions. Here, the exposed upper shelves show off framed artwork and a few well-chosen dishes—you'd hardly even recognize it as storage, per se. Meanwhile, below deck, pretty, alphabet-printed fabric cloaks not just the area under the sink, but a whole wall's worth of cleaning products and cooking pots. The dining table's long white linen cloth echoes the skirted sink, but creates a feeling of calm and reflects more light from the white floors and walls.

Below: With its chicken-wire-paneled doors (an easy DIY revamp), matte gray paint job, and orderly rows of gleaming, gold-trimmed glassware, this eight-foot cupboard is the picture of refined rusticity. All the less-glitzy necessities take cover behind a curtain of gathered canvas drop cloth staple-gunned inside the cabinet's lower doors.

Take Pride of Plates

Arrayed on open shelves or harbored in a hutch, your tableware can help set the scene. And there's a way to make it work no matter what kind of collection you have. Solid colors may be the most foolproof to display—go for a matching cupboard or shelves for a seamless, sculptural effect and group similar shapes together to make things look considered. For everything else, incorporate some purely decorative details to enliven the look (and keep it from seeming overly utilitarian).

bright idea!

Centered on a shallow ledge, the wide white platter almost reads as an architectural element.

Left: The simple abundance of dozens of ivory dishes and bowls all in a row evokes a classical relief carving. It's hard to imagine a more striking assemblage—or a more convenient place to stash plates.

Left: Stocking an open rolling rack (this one once served as a shoe-factory display) with casual dishes, pitchers, and utensils conveys a "help yourself" ethos (great for a household that sees a lot of guests). The loose, colorful arrangement is made even more accessible by the addition of a few conversation pieces (framed butterflies, a folk-art face jug) and an unusual potted plant.

Right: Consider it a study in contrasts: The timeworn wood of this antique case highlights the flawless finish of an assortment of all-white serving pieces—which reads as a set, thanks to the uniform hue.

ANATOMY OF AN ORGANIZED DINING ROOM

With freestanding furniture pieces that deliver both structure and storage, and a show-and-tell approach to serving pieces, this dining room satisfies on every level.

1. Aim high. The top of the hutch can hold just as much as (and actually a little bit more than) any of its shelves.

2. The white walls, white accents, and high ceiling keep the dark-colored cupboards from feeling too heavy, while the black-and-white artwork ties the room's elements together.

3. Two sideboards are better than one. A matched pair flanking a tall hutch (all custom made by Amish artisans) amps up the storage capacity and adds symmetry and structure to the angled-roof room.

4. Baskets fill the free space beneath the sideboards and make a discreet place to toss soiled table linens awaiting a washing.

5. The homeowner's own art pottery, emblazoned with dictionary-like drawings of flora and fauna, populates a highly functional cabinet of (not-just) curiosities.

Don't Skip the Small Stuff

After you've loaded up your larger storage pieces, start seeking out less-obvious openings. Drawers, ledges, and cubbies can complement cupboards and cabinetry and put frequently used staples within easy reach—or keep occasion-specific items out of the fray.

Once you switch to a table with built-in drawers (ideal for flatware and serving utensils), you'll wonder how you ever settled for less. Your best bet for finding one: Seek out repurposed desks or industrial tables (this one hails from a florist's shop).

Vintage breadboxes perched on a high shelf take extra table linens and party and picnic supplies up, up, and away. Positioning the shelf well above the windows (rather than right on top of them) and painting it a light color that matches the walls wards off unwanted shadows.

Raise the Bar

Having a dedicated space to pour guests a drink lets you ease into even the most impromptu of entertaining situations. The secret is distilling what you need down to the very essence, then concocting a stylish setup that can live out in the open all the time (or be easily accessed and tucked away again as needed). Rolling carts (both traditional and with a twist) do the job nicely, and freestanding furniture can be sliced into segments to suit your needs. Even an orphaned dresser drawer can be drafted into service!

For a minimalist bar like this one, editing is everything. Leave out only the best-looking stuff (both spirits and stemware), and hide backstock, tools, and humbler tumblers in the cabinets.

This wheeled iron number has ample inner compartments for tea towels and cocktail napkins and enough surface area for more than one amateur mixologist to work at once. Plus, it's easy to reposition for—or during—parties.

bright idea!
A sealed canister keeps kitchen matches dry.

Above: Carving out an entertainment station in a corner of a dining room is just this simple: Set out a tray of spirits and some glasses. Add a robust record collection (CDs work, too). Provide a chair from which to peruse them. Done!

Left: A potting bench equipped with barware, plates, and a perky bouquet turns any patio into garden-party central. Stacks of durable melamine dishes, a crate of surplus bottles, and a stash of candles corralled in a lantern occupy the bottom level, while a topple-proof punch dispenser anchors the top shelf.

HOMEWORK

Upcycle a dresser drawer into a sublime drink station.

Here's how to make a hide-and-chic mini bar that disappears after last call.

1. Measure the inside of a dresser drawer and use a jigsaw to cut one piece of wood for a vertical divider and one for a shelf (as shown). Sand the ends.

2. Using this photo as a guide, insert the shelf and divider into the drawer; screw in place with a drill.

3. To create the drop-down door, remove any screws holding the dresser's top to its frame; then pop the top off the frame using a rubber mallet.

4. Paint the drawer unit and door if desired, then let dry.

5. Stand the drawer so that the front faces up and its open top faces you. Following package instructions for a piano hinge, attach the door to the back edge of the drawer, as shown above.

6. Using our photo as a guide, screw in a set of eye bolts inside the drawer's sides, about three inches from the drawer's front and ½ inch from the top. Use pliers and eye hooks to attach a length of ¼-inch-wide chain to each eye bolt. Then, on each side of the door, about two inches down from the top edge and ½ inch in from the sides, drill a hole ¾ inch wide.

7. Position the door at a 90-degree angle and pull each chain to meet the hole in the door, then remove excess chain with pliers. Insert each chain's last link into its respective door hole, then drive a screw into the door's side and into the hole, threading the link onto the screw as you go.

8. To keep the door shut, install safety-gate hooks-and-eyes on the outside of the door and drawer, as shown above. Finish by installing a drawer pull in the center of the drawer's front; then use mounting brackets to hang the station on a wall.

Uncluttered Kitchens

More than any other room in the house, the kitchen thrives on practicality, utility, and order, and a solid organizational system is a must. But just because this hardworking space needs to be functional doesn't mean it can't be appealing, too. Assembling a kitchen that suits your needs—and your tastes—is a little like perfecting a new recipe. You start with the basics—a sturdy island here, a hanging pot rail there—and mix in other elements as the mood strikes. How about a baker's rack in that corner for keeping everyday dishes within arm's reach? And why not repurpose an antique icebox as a pantry for surplus non-perishables? In every instance, the ideas in this chapter aim higher than merely facilitating tidy cupboards and clear countertops. They strive for warmth as well as efficiency, and celebrate abundance in all its forms—even when that means having to find a place for one more hand-glazed pie bird or transferware teapot. Smart space-savers and streamlined setups may be an organized kitchen's bread and butter, but it's the dashes of improvisation and innovation you contribute that provide the spice.

< Special-occasion serving pieces—cake stands, covered platters, and the like—get the top-shelf treatment in this floor-to-ceiling built-in. The glossy-black rolling library ladder, while practical, is also the room's punctuation mark.

Shop Outside the Kitchen Store

Sure, some folks dream of a kitchen that could've been ripped from a catalog—all stainless-steel precision and vacant countertops. But if, like us, you prefer something a little less cookie-cutter, try furnishing your kitchen with flexible finds from the flea market, the antique store, and the hardware aisle. A writing desk, school locker, or amped-up armoire may be just the secret ingredient you've been looking for.

Score one for the home team! Wood-and-glass lockers salvaged from an old school make winning holders for glassware and dishes—while also capitalizing on the available vertical space. Encased inside a white-painted lumber framework, they feel like part of the room's architecture.

MEAT MARKET

A midcentury grocer's scale and a two-tiered wheeled cart keep dish towels and table linens at the ready—and the scale's dial echoes the time-worn clock face behind it. Together, the rounded shapes and roughed-up surfaces lend this converted loft a cozy feel.

GAZ
A TOUS LES ÉTAGES

In this Tennessee retreat, an outdated zinc icebox stores dry goods, while open Douglas-fir shelves hold dishes and cookware. Underscoring the intersection of cottage and industry: a retired metal worktable topped with custom-cut glass, which doubles as an island and a place to keep oversized pots.

bright idea!
Add metal label holders to identify an array of keys.

Above: Tricked out with a key rack, a basket for mail and delivery menus, and a message board for family reminders, a basic hutch becomes an all-purpose service station for daily necessities.

Right: This antique writing table reads as thoroughly culinary when positioned in the kitchen and equipped with a couple of produce crates and a crock for utensils. The lower shelf was created by propping planks across the stretchers.

A consistent color palette makes this pair of stacked pale-green boxes seem like an extension of the cabinetry. Another built-in boon? The deep bay-style window ledge, which supplies an easy-access perch for pitchers and pots.

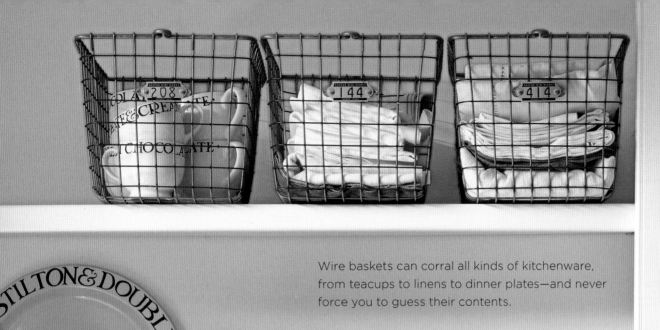

Wire baskets can corral all kinds of kitchenware, from teacups to linens to dinner plates—and never force you to guess their contents.

ANATOMY OF AN ORGANIZED KITCHEN

One highly functional (and completely unique) kitchen—with lessons anyone can borrow.

1. Wooden crates pay homage to area farms—and organize supplies.

2. Clad in faux-wood adhesive paneling, this zinc-topped island conceals compact appli-ances—refrigerator draw-ers, a dishwasher, and a microwave.

3. Regardless of prov-enance, ivory dishes always look good enough to live out in the open.

4. File this under fabulous: An antique hardware-store cabinet takes the place of built-ins, providing shelves for dishware and copious compartments for utensils, tools, and even recipe cards.

5. Rack 'em up! A shallow, nearly floor-to-ceiling niche stores and displays oversize platters and a sentimental Mississippi-shaped cutting board—but claims a tiny footprint.

6. Declare your (storage) intentions. Typed labels on the hardware-store cabinet's drawers reveal what's hidden inside.

7. Talk about a pipe dream realized. Black-and-white shelves constructed from humble hardware-store materials could pass for more-expensive industrial-chic designs.

Invest In Smart Space-Savers

Has anyone ever complained about having too much room to cook? We didn't think so. But even in a big kitchen, every inch counts—especially when that copper-pot collection keeps bubbling over. Why not try one of these clever economizers on for size?

A trompe l'oeil shelf designed to look like a window valance brings brightly colored vessels out of the shadows—and barely blocks any daylight in the process. Beneath it, a pair of hooks holds colanders and measuring cups.

Right: Wall-to-wall cabinetry can overwhelm a pint-sized space—so this homeowner opted for a compact, custom-made plate rack. Removing the room's dropped ceiling also opened up opportunities for stacking bowls on the rack's top.

Below: Going for an extra wide island may seem counterintuitive, but this one's partially open design permits stools to be stowed beneath it between uses.

bright idea!
Install a small plate rack on the side of a kitchen island.

Coat hooks aren't just for jackets: A small two-pronged number can be posted almost anywhere to hoist canisters, jugs, water bottles, and more.

Turn your under-cabinets into overachievers with these two easy upgrades: First, install a sliding shelf using drawer guides and plywood to support a hidden trash can. Then, affix clothespins to the inside of the door (using adhesive-backed Velcro or magnets) to keep tabs on unsightly rubber gloves, sponges, and shopping bags.

A row of mug hooks puts both the top and the bottom of a shelf to good use—and facilitates showing off an attractive collection, as in the case of these 1950s jadeite pieces.

Free up space in the
spice rack—and encour-
age tableside snipping—
by growing fresh herbs
in wall-mounted planters.

Where others might see obstacles, these homeowners registered only opportunities—and took advantage of every one. The oft-overlooked space under the angled roof rises to the challenge of storing dishes and appliances, while mug hooks and a plate rack mounted below elevate their respective contents. Colorful cookware hangs proudly on the wall in a graphic display of ingenuity, and a window-spanning ledge handily proffers condiments.

ADD PERSONALITY

Giving off-the-rack cabinets custom allure is all in the details. Here are four ideas for sprucing up the old standbys.

SWAP OUT THE HARDWARE. Delightful drawer pulls (like the skeleton-key style, right) unlock a new kitchen look—fast. Contemporary and antique versions abound, and it's a snap to make your own out of found objects (straps of leather, knotted rope, champagne corks) or diminutive collectibles (figurines, fancy buttons, mismatched flatware).

TRANSFORM THE DOORS WITH PAINT... Choose a cheery hue and a high-gloss latex formula (for less-toxic fumes and easier upkeep). Don't forget to clean well with a degreaser first, then sand and prime the surfaces before brushing on color.

...OR APPLY WALLPAPER FOR A TEMPORARY FIX... Removable, self-adhesive wallpaper delivers no-commitment panache. (Stick to just the raised or recessed center panels at the front of the door for easier application.)

OR REPLACE THE DOORS ENTIRELY. Los Angeles-based company Semihandmade (semihandmadedoors.com) turns out high-quality doors and drawer fronts for practically every Ikea cabinet model—at a fraction of the price of a fully-custom job.

TAKE A NUMBER. In brass, wood, or porcelain (as seen here), vintage number plates can impart aged appeal to new china cabinets and cupboards.

One Essential Trick:
Go For Open Shelving

A surefire strategy for making any kitchen seem more spacious? Forgo upper cabinets in favor of open shelving. Done right, it turns your tableware into an appealing tableau, while—and here's the real beauty—making it easy for houseguests and other helpers to pull out or put away their own dishes. These four examples demonstrate the versatility of this approach.

Stuff them to the gills. Shorter shelf heights allow for more—and more-functional—stacks, especially when they span the whole distance from countertop to ceiling. Matching the trim to the mostly-white dishes reins in the chaos.

Top Left: Curate an artful display. Integrating vintage knickknacks—a wooden Pepsi caddy, 1970s cookbooks, and a drawer sporting an ad for Drummond's Horse Shoe tobacco—with everyday dishware enhances both. The shelves themselves, painted to match the walls, visually recede.

Top right: Take it to go. Throwback baker's racks can pick up the slack when traditional storage options are in short supply. Wheel them anywhere for a smart vertical solution that demands very little square footage.

Bottom left: Draw the eye up. A tiered system with staggered shelf depths adds visual interest, and the chalkboard wall behind it supplies both eye-catching contrast and a place for silly doodles and recipe reminders.

Tend to Your Tools

The hardest-working cooking implements can also be the toughest to tuck away. (We're looking at you, potato masher!) Stop trying to cram them into cluttered drawers and adopt a few of these tried-and-true alternatives.

Left: Tea towels this pretty should never be hidden in a closet. Instead, try a wall-mounted wire rack with a feminine curlicued rim.

Above: Hung vertically, a pair of ordinary peg-style coat racks give rolling pins a boost.

A small peg shelf and a few well-placed nails turn a collection of color-coordinated (but awkwardly shaped) tools into a charming vignette. Completing the scene: a row of small Italian ceramic herb jars lined up along the ledge.

bright idea!
Simple S hooks turn a pipe
into a pot rack.

Opposite: It's all systems go in this no-nonsense galley: A sky-high pipe holds pots aloft; silverware stands at attention in a rustic wood caddy; a wall-mounted magnetic strip collects cutlery; and small appliances have just enough room to stay out under the open shelves. Beneath the redwood farm table, crates and bins gather dry goods and hardy produce.

Right: You don't need a fancy store-bought system to keep your flatware in top form. Mix-and-match baskets and trays can be removed one at a time and reconfigured endlessly.

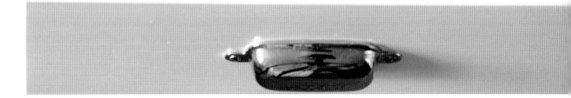

All it takes to jazz up a basic knife block is a pencil and some paint. After carefully tracing the outlines of the knives you'll nestle inside, paint the block's background one color and the "blades" another. Voila—one cutting-edge kitchen accessory.

Stitch up a pretty fabric pouch

A neater kitchen is in the bag—with these easy-to-make catchalls.

1. First, create a pattern. Cut a piece of paper or scrap fabric into a 7-by-10-inch rectangle, then cut one of the 7-inch edges into a rounded shape.

2. Using the pattern, cut four pieces of fabric: two from one printed fabric and two from another. Sew the contrasting pieces together with the right sides facing out. Select the fabric for the outside of the bag, and turn the pieces so that that side faces in. Line up and sew the two halves together, leaving the top open.

3. Turn the bag right side out and turn over a one-inch cuff of the contrasting fabric.

4. Punch holes in the fabric and apply grommets following the instructions included with a grommet kit.

5. Hang with S hooks.

Polish Up the Pantry

Charming containers and user-friendly accessories turn your nonperishables into a feast for the eyes (and save you time gathering the ingredients for dinner). Plus: Three ways to reinvent the spice rack.

Why hide nature's beautiful bounty? Blueberry crates mounted on a wall seem destined for storing pantry staples—they're precisely one canning jar deep. Nearby, a stylish side table supports a portable herb garden in a wire caddy that easily travels outside for sunning sessions.

Left: Have a spare corner? Then you can carve out a small (but highly serviceable) pantry, using just a tall L-shaped unit, like this one from Williams-Sonoma. The heaviest items in the largest containers (think water jugs and sacks of spuds) will find a natural—and stability-reinforcing—home on the lowest shelf.

Above right: The answer for high, deep shelves that seem to swallow whatever gets pushed to the back? Labeled wood crates (simple chalk does the trick) that you can pull out and rifle through at eye level.

Above: An old-fashioned ironing-board cabinet is just deep enough to store spice jars. Replace the board with a few narrow shelves and you're all set.

Left: A flea-market painting that just fits around a medicine cabinet's mirror (or plain metal front) recasts it as a covert cupboard for the smallest canisters.

Another option for unconventional ingredients storage? A vintage medicine chest for herbs and seasonings, paired with a matching toolbox for bulk refills.

When pantry staples are decanted into good-looking vessels, they can become part of the décor. Just remember to unify the rest of the room with a consistent color scheme—pairing white with wood rarely goes wrong—and weed out any unnecessary extras.

UPGRADE WITH LABELS

Three ways to gussy up glass jars.

Below: Empty lemonade bottles are reborn as cruets when outfitted with cork pourers and slate tags. Below them, a row of old canning jars gain some culinary cachet courtesy of vintage-inspired French labels.

Top right: Sweeten up baking supplies with transparent sticker sheets printed with cross-stitch-inspired lettering. (You can download the Home Sweet Home font for free on myfonts.com.)

Bottom right: Erasable chalkboard decals make it easy to keep track of snacks—and to swap out the jars' contents as needed.

bright idea!
Turn any chair int
functional office
seating—with a who
lot more panache
than a standard
roller seat—by ada
ing casters to its le

Inspiring Home Offices & Creative Spaces

Establishing a workspace that's just for you—whether it's a home office, a DIY design studio, or a craft room for creative unwinding—can be a real sanity-saver, not to mention a reliable way to keep paperwork and pompoms from creeping out into other parts of the house. Think you don't have room? Consider this: some of the most inspiring examples we've seen occupy the unlikeliest spaces, from a corner of a busy kitchen to a free wall in a mudroom—and even inside a bedroom closet. Wherever in the home they're found, each of the workspaces featured in this chapter is built around clutter-taming tactics (you'll insist on a flip-top desk henceforth) and dirt-cheap DIY ideas for one-of-a-kind filing systems and supply storage. And each boasts colorful personal touches galore. All work and no play? It's time to retire that idea for good.

< Towering file cubbies on either side of the desk make room for more inspiring views front and center—a collection of mustard-yellow McCoy pottery and a small portrait, both set off by a backdrop of pretty, green-and-white wallpaper.

Carve Out a Niche

Almost any area in your home—no matter how big or small—can be converted into a successful workspace. It's all about taking inventory of your needs (a big table, ample sunlight, or a genius filing system, say) and "shopping" around the house for slivers of real estate—and the tools to transform it.

A mudroom may seem like an odd place to construct a workspace, but it's actually ideal for catching and filing incoming mail and paperwork straight away. The bar-height pine table becomes an ace replacement for a desk when complemented with a pair of comfortable stools.

Even a Lilliputian chunk of hallway can become an office with smart, out-of-the-way storage (like this single upper cabinet borrowed from the kitchen) and a low-profile desk that's just large enough for paying bills. A crocheted seat cover softens the scene.

Because schedules need organizing, too—a family-sized chalkboard calendar on a kitchen wall takes a playful approach to plotting out the daily grind. A $10 yard-sale door, set atop two $8 wooden brackets, serves as a desk.

The magic formula for making homework (or tax forms) disappear? A super-slim wall-mounted metal desk that folds up when your work is done. Add artwork to its outside surface with magnets to really change the mood in a snap, and opt for a chic chair that can fit in as occasional seating elsewhere in the house.

A row of secondhand filing cabinets—spray-painted sunny yellow and topped with a plywood plank—adds up to an out-of-this-world filing solution and a clever perch for thrift-store globes.

ANATOMY OF AN ORGANIZED OFFICE

Talk about a corner office! Outfitted with a DIY desk, multipurpose door panels, and a few girly accessories, this two-by-six-foot closet becomes a vibrant work space blooming with inspiration.

1. A readymade melamine tabletop and a pair of wheeled stands turn two standard metal file cabinets into a modular, moveable desk.

2. To keep odds and ends from engulfing your desktop, take advantage of unused space on the insides of the closet's doors. Cut pegboard and cork to your desired dimensions. Screw the pegboard and cork into place, and frame with wood trim. The final step: Paint the inner doors.

3. Avoid the visual clutter of brackets and hardware with floating planks; they don't overwhelm the tiny room—or obscure too much of the floral-print wallpaper.

4. Why buy humdrum office supplies when storage boxes come in pretty prints, and you can use almost any vessel (cups, vases, trophies) to corral pencils, paper clips, and the like?

5. A dainty chandelier delivers more elegance than the usual overhead fixtures, while a desk lamp offers task lighting.

6. Casters and an adjustable seat enable this feminine, wicker-and-metal chair to slide all the way under the desk at day's end.

Tame the Clutter

Even if you're an alphabet away from Type A, tidiness can be yours (and it doesn't have to come at the expense of individuality). All kinds of objects can keep office supplies in check—from jazzed-up shoe boxes to antique flower frogs.

A hideaway desk—especially one with a back-tilting lid—packs serious mess-masking potential. Use wood glue to attach a corkboard inside the desk's top panel for holding swatches, sketches, and reminders, then subdivide the interior space with an assortment of attractive containers. Here, a flower frog grounds a bouquet of pencils, glass jars show off colorful tape and decorative pushpins, and an earthy ceramic bowl holds business cards awaiting attention.

Make snazzy, stackable safes for travel treasures.

Swap the scrapbook for a three-dimensional repository for vacation mementos like photos, postcards, menus, matchbooks, and coins—which might otherwise get lost in a junk drawer. You'll want to unpack it again and again.

1. Trace the silhouette of the city, state, country, or continent you visited onto a paper map of the destination. For variety, consider all types of cartography: topographic maps, subway-line diagrams, and other kinds of guides.

2. Cut out the shape and paste it onto the lid of a plain white box.

3. Finish with an adhesive label showing the date of your journey.

4. Commence reminiscing.

A motley crew of cardboard boxes makes a unified statement when sheathed in old maps and newspapers (use foreign ones for even more élan). Label each one to know just where to turn for craft supplies, stapler refills, or pay stubs.

TOOLS

VENICE

SILVER TEA PAPER

ITALIAN PAPER

CHALK PASTEL

VENICE

OIL PASTEL

TOOLS

BLACK RIBBON

BROWN RIBBON

PINK RIBBON

RED RIBBON

FOILS

METALLIC/NEUTRAL RIBBON

GREEN RIBBON

ORANGE RIBBON

BLUE RIBBON

BEAD/SEQUINS

COLOURS

CHALKS

GLITTER

GOLD BULION/TINSEL

SILVER BULLION/TINSEL

COLOURED METALLIC THREAD

FRENCH TEXT

GOLD BULLION

FEATHERS

RUBBER STAMPS

GLITTER

BIG ALPHABET

PAPER

ODDS & ENDS

PORTRAITS of NOTICES HISTORIQU PAR M. MIGNET

CAMERA

SAMPLES

PHOTOS

LETT

In a plethora of shapes and sizes—and emblazoned with colorful graphics and cool throwback typography—vintage tins and canisters can catch all kinds of everyday items, from writing utensils to mailing labels. (Save the lids for those objects you don't want gathering dust.)

ADOPT SOME HOLDING PATTERNS

Seven strategies for getting a grip on small-scale craft and office supplies.

1. Stack tape refills around a countertop paper towel rod.

2. Repurpose a silverware tray to bring order to colored pencils, markers, pens, and paintbrushes.

3. Keep business cards in a pretty recipe-card file.

4. Use vintage teacups to hold paperclips and push pins.

5. Load spools of thread, or replacement shirt buttons, inside a lidded glass compote or terrarium.

6. Pile colorful balls of yarn in a hanging wire produce basket, or use a glass cloche to showcase them as sculpture (also jewelry) (as shown below).

7. Separate jewelry findings, beads, or spare buttons in a day-of-the-week pill container.

What a catch! A bright-red enamel tackle box brings order—and a bold pop of color—to a diminutive desk space. Another reason to reel one of these in? Your office becomes instantly portable, so you can drift wherever the day takes you.

Add a sly security detail to plain wood boxes by applying trompe l'oeil padlocks, latches, and name-plates (along with some safety-orange paint). Simply photocopy actual hardware, affix the images to the container's surface with glue, and finish with a couple coats of Mod Podge (allowing 20 minutes drying time between coats).

Use the same technique to whip up carbon-copy containers for tacks, scissors, and pencils and keep your work station looking extra sharp.

Get Crafty

There's no better place to experiment with one-of-a-kind organizing tactics than in a craft room—your most whimsical, imaginative space. (Plus, all those paint-brushes, stamps, and sewing notions can easily morph from inspiring treasure trove to overwhelming mess if you're not careful.) Consider these fun and offbeat ideas the warm-up to your artistic main event.

Repurpose hardware-store paint swatches in seconds flat: Simply stack two same-size cards atop each other, right sides facing out, and stitch together along the bottoms and sides with contrasting thread. Then use flathead tacks to attach your brilliant little pocket organizers to a bulletin board, and fill them with pencils, papers, and more.

This pantry cabinet houses a cornucopia of crafting ingredients on its adjustable shelves. Shallow trays on top and underneath further reduce the need for rummaging.

Vibrant skeins of yarn approach pop-sculptural status when arrayed on the wall on individual hooks (instead of stuffed away in a bin). The display constantly evolves as projects are completed, and duplicate colors await use in the desk's hollow supports. Fabric scraps, liberated from craft-closet obscurity, stay wrinkle-free on a standing steel magazine rack.

Left: How to store material goods in style: Stash bolts of fabric in an industrial trash can and skewer swatches on giant safety pins.

Opposite: How do we love this design studio built for two? Let us count the ways. There's the pair of matching cabinets that provide symmetry while doubling the storage; the standing floor lamps that keep the tabletop clear; and the genius way a hollow box custom-made to top two identical consoles raised the surface to counter height (so the designers can work while standing). Even the slim space between the windows is busy holding a pin cushion.

bright idea!
A roll of kraft paper mounted to the side of the desk turns the surface into a giant sketch pad at a moment's notice.

Streamlined Washrooms

A beautiful bathroom with pristine countertops and towels stacked just so. A zen-like laundry area featuring matching baskets and plenty of space for folding and sorting. A linen closet stocked with orderly sheet sets and nary a stray pillowcase. Forget long-stemmed roses and walks on the beach—these are the fantasies that drift through our minds on a daily basis. Fortunately, these earthly delights don't have to remain a mere wash-daydream. Achieving that spa-like, sanctuary feel is largely a matter of stripping down (ditching ugly product packaging in favor of coordinated containers), amping up storage potential (by bringing in extra furniture, baskets, and bins), and devising clever ways to keep cosmetics, backup bath supplies, and the contents of your medicine cabinet under wraps. Here's to making a clean sweep!

< Modern conveniences don't have to mean boring bathrooms. Here, a 1910 medicine cabinet moves into the 21st century thanks to a new mirror, and a weathered table (with a drawer for cosmetics or hair styling tools) does a stand-up job holding a sink. Its wide marble top also has plenty of room for anything good-looking enough to leave out.

Reimagine the Medicine Cabinet

A fresh take on the medicine chest—keeper of your beauty secrets and also one of the first things you see each day—may be just what the doctor ordered for reinvigorating your morning routine. (Consider it the cure for common bathroom storage.)

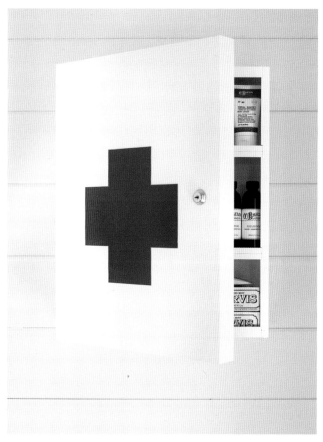

A no-frills cross cut from red magnetic sheeting transforms a guest bath's utilitarian metal locker into a cute conversation piece.

No, it's not technically a medicine cabinet. But this dynamic duo of a tri-fold shaving mirror and narrow wire shelf make a convincing case for thinking outside the box. Anything too bulky for the slim platform can find a home inside the antique table below.

When open, the space-saving sliding doors of this model give access to a generous recessed medicine chest. Closed, they make the whole cubby disappear—which has the happy added benefit of discouraging nosy visitors from poking around.

Lacking bathroom storage? This adorable up-cycle will have you covered

If you don't have a linen closet, the space underneath your sink or vanity—or underneath a repurposed sde table or desk—can double as storage for towels, shower curtains, or even sheets.

HOMEWORK

1. Purchase a cafe-curtain tension rod that fits the width of your vanity or side table.

2. Cut fabric to desired length, adding on two inches in length for the hems (and another inch or two if you'd like the skirt to puddle).

3. Sew a loop pocket along the top edge of the fabric, and hem the opposite edge.

4. Slip the curtain rod through the pocket and position it under the countertop.

5. For even more coverage, repeat for the other exposed sides of the table.

DISPENSE WITH FORMALITY

Bringing harmony to your vanity is as simple as transferring toiletries into pretty, coordinated receptacles (which can be scored for a song at flea markets, junk shops, and kitchen-supply stores).

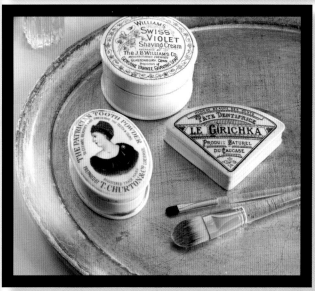

Above: Lovely labels and a mirrored tray turn plain glass vinegar bottles—bought in bulk for less than a buck apiece—into vanity-worthy vessels.

Above: Glass-stoppered apothecary bottles dole out Epsom salts, talcum powder, and other dry goods with antique flair.

Bottom: You can avoid advertising the contents of your medicine cabinet when you stock up on delightfully discreet 19th-century ceramic toiletry containers.

Enlist Ledges

As useful as shelving (without any of the visual weight), a ledge gives myriad beauty tools and treatments a handy place to land—anywhere you need them. For a subtle look, install ledges throughout the room (atop beadboard panels or wainscoting), but limit yourself to a few clusters of goods here and there, keeping the other areas free.

Leaning this mirror on a ledge eliminated the need for a run-of-the-mill medicine cabinet, especially since the repurposed sideboard-turned-washstand beneath it can hold so much. (And all the countertop clutter can be cleared away in a flash when company's coming.)

A crystal-clear chandelier and a few large pieces of art balance out this washroom's casual hodgepodge of storage ideas: bath products on the ledge, towels stacked on a stool, and a tray of toilet-paper rolls atop the tank.

Cast Some Guest Stars

Pieces of furniture pulled from other areas of the house can amp up the bathroom's utility—and appeal. Stuck with a cramped w.c.? The smartest space-saving solution may already be in your mudroom, in the form of a slim storage bench. Or, if you have square footage to spare, don't waste it. The powder room can hold more than towels and toiletries, after all. Bring in a wardrobe, dresser, or trunk, and voila: instant dressing room.

Positioned near the tub, an old mailbox gets a second career as a bath holder.

Yes, you can have it both ways: This embellished antique cabinet hides cleaning supplies, toilet paper, and cosmetics, while the spare, streamlined sink stand preserves a feeling of openness.

An antique medical stand acts as a convenient holder for hand towels, while a cache of vintage Ukrainian newspapers becomes a graphic wall covering with the help of wallpaper paste and a flat craft sealant. Wall-mounted cubbies supply extra (extra!) storage for items that don't fit in the medicine chest.

Adding drama to a bathroom need not be a merely decorative endeavor. Here, an elegantly sloping coat rack cuts a striking figure while holding robes, towels, and jewelry at the ready.

Left: You may have retired that rickety wooden ladder from real feats of strength, but it can easily elevate (and air out) towels near the tub. (It's your very own leaning tower of pima!)

Below: To create a natty hamper that doubles as a stool, simply spruce up a wooden box with paint and insert a pair of removable his-and-hers laundry baskets or totes.

LAND DEEDS

- Queen's Bench Division -

A tall, dark, and handsome lacquer cabinet (topped with matching black tin traveling trunks) brings some old-world romance to an otherwise modern washroom—and turns a shallow nook into a full-fledged dressing area, complete with a settee for lounging.

Above left: Assorted bath-supply surplus finds a suitable home within a repurposed riding-boot chest that started out in a stable.

Above right: Two sink basins plus two mirrors plus one old chest of drawers equals an infinite improvement over sharing a single primp station with multiple family members. It doubles the surface area, the hidden storage—and the elbow room, come toothbrushing time.

Left: A few coats of hard-wearing Rust-Oleum paint gave a ramshackle assortment of castoffs—a flea-market chest, a secondhand mirror, and a shelf made from fragments of an old dresser—the look of a matched set.

One Essential Trick: Embrace Baskets

In wood, wicker, rattan, or wire, baskets really hold their own in a bathroom (and can be repurposed endlessly throughout the house). Use a few to fill in for an absent linen closet or medicine cabinet—or anywhere else you could use a hand(le).

Solving a common problem of freestanding tubs—little or no ledge space—a bath-side basket proffers towels while a woven ottoman-turned-side table supports toiletries.

Above left: Tucking towels in baskets rather than in cupboards is more casual (and houseguest-friendly, since they'll never have to hunt for one). The bins also excel at obscuring exposed pipes.

Above right: Extending the full length of the wall, a single long shelf accommodates two roomy crates and echoes the horizontally-hung knotty pine wall planks and slab-like vanity. The parallel lines create a clean, rustic-meets-minimalist look.

Left: A rack of open wire cubbies delivers more storage than a medicine chest, and fabric-lined bins catch the bits and bobs that might otherwise slip through the cracks.

ANATOMY OF AN ORGANIZED LINEN CLOSET

No built-in storage? No problem. An ordinary armoire, tricked out with paint, hooks, trays, and bins, makes a dashing solution for keeping bedding and bathroom supplies in order.

1. Keep necessities out of sight—not out of mind. Lined bins conceal cleaning supplies and toilet paper, but stamped tags ensure that one's are perfectly clear.

2. Give sheets the gift treatment. Pretty ribbon solves the lost-pillowcase conundrum and offers a polished presentation. Metal labels distinguish the twins from the fulls and queens.

3. Handled trays collect easy-to-tote amenities that move from closet to bathroom with grace. And gathering cotton balls and q-tips in glass jars renders them almost luxurious.

4. Designate a landing space for bulky spare pillows. A drop-front basket tucked inside a low shelf is ideal.

5. Put brackets to genius new use. These iron beauties deftly divide shelves into separate units.

bright idea!

The key to milking every square inch? A nimble under-shelf bin that takes advantage of oft-wasted space. Use it as a spot to store a stack of washcloths, hand towels, or extra pillowcases.

TOILET PAPER

LAUNDRY PRODUCTS

CLEANING SUPPLIES

QUEEN

FULL

TWIN

Freshen Up the Laundry Room

Sure, we've come a long way from washtubs and clotheslines (although we still thrill to the smell of air-dried linens). But even modern laundry rooms tend to end up littered with leaky detergent bottles, stray clothes pins, and orphaned socks. Here's how to straighten up and dry right.

Who says laundry has to be sorted in uninspiring plastic hampers? Woven baskets do the same job—and imbue the workaday space with a more homey vibe.

Above left: As with toiletries and other bathroom supplies, laundry-room essentials get a beautiful boost when transferred to pretty vintage containers.

Above right: A wooden domicile for dolls, recast as a wall-mounted cleaning-supply cubby, gives new meaning to the phrase "playing house." Shapely brackets up the whimsy factor (while facilitating the storage of heavier items).

Left: Now here's a slide show worth seeing: A customized ironing board drawer that glides cleanly out of the way when the pressing's complete.

Order Indoors & Out

The in-between spaces of a home—the porch, the patio, the mudroom, the garage—are vital stations in the course of a day's activities, but also tend to be landing places (aka clutter traps) for all kinds of quickly cast-off stuff. Maintaining order calls for vigilance, but establishing some smart systems can also go a long way toward creating appealing entrances, efficient working areas, and inviting outdoor "rooms" that thrive with minimal effort. It's all about planting the seeds for easy passage: carving out space for odd-shaped and bulky items, designating drop zones for everyday gear, and unearthing unconventional storage opportunities (like adorning an exterior wall with watering cans and gardening tools). The end result? Welcoming, wide-open spaces that make an impeccable first (or last) impression.

< A trough brimming with firewood and a crew of oars assembled in a barrel turn an alfresco sitting area into a poetic lakeside scene. Simple enamel buckets make for cachepots with laid-back charm (and also play off their larger, galvanized-metal brethren).

Maximize the Mudroom

More than a place to shed your coat and boots, a well-planned mudroom or entry-way can set you up for success and smooth the transition between home and the outside world. Say goodbye to misplaced keys and lost umbrellas and hello to many happy returns.

One way to address your family's organizational issues? Call on a second-hand mail-room filing cabinet to divide and conquer hats, mittens, sunglasses, spare keys, and yes, correspondence and catalogs.

Chickenwire meets chinoiserie in this high-contrast, high-impact entryway. A pair of slim sentries shelters outerwear, while supporting a set of shapely vases. As for that vivid crimson wall covering? Think of it as a cheeky twist on rolling out the red carpet for all your very special guests.

A colorful bench and an antique lobster-shack sign enliven this multigenerational family retreat's vibrant vestibule. Plentiful pegs hoist hats and jackets and a picnic kit (with basket and blankets) claims a grab-and-go perch. Don't fret: The space doesn't have to be spotless, as long as there's a general destination for all the detritus that flows through (as in: shoes under the bench, bags atop it).

Top Left: "Mom, where's my...?" questions stop in their tracks when openwork wire baskets are tasked with catching sporting equipment and favorite toys near the front door.

Top right: The outdoor equivalent of those wire bins: A striped wooden barrel that provides poolside storage with nautical flair.

Bottom left: Installing a floating shoe cubby allows for easier routine floor cleaning and keeps footwear pileup in check.

Left: A truly clever choice for hallway storage? Rugged metal lockers that maximize vertical space while hiding clutter. The three separate compartments, handy hooks, and adjustable shelves make it easy to ensure that everyone leaves for the day with what they need and puts it away again upon their return.

Opposite: Like a green room for gardeners, this farmhouse sink-equipped way station occupies the (cutting) edge between indoors and out. Wire crates beneath the work table corral casual vases and canning jars for on-the-spot arrangements, while enamel bowls on the upper shelf offer hand towels and soaps for cleaning soil-caked hands.

POOL

SOAPS   TOILETRIES

bright idea!
Ornate brackets turn reclaimed
lumber into a stylish shelf.

SINCE 1876

ANHEUSER-BUSCH INC.
&
PROPERTY
ST. LOUIS, MO.

ANHEUSER-BUSCH INC.
PROPERTY
ST. LOUIS, MO.

Hook Smart

A coat rack is one way to do it. But it's not the only way. These three inventive ideas show that you can hang your hat—and your parka, trench, and barn jackets—almost anywhere.

Wall-mounted antlers buck convention when employed to hold lightweight straw hats.

A rescued wood plank adorned with hardware-store hooks reads as artfully distressed, when paired with a handmade fir bench and rugged baskets.

Simultaneously edgy and earthy, this brick-red entryway gains organic appeal from an undulating row of DIY twig hooks. To make them, use a handsaw to slice branches down one side—so they'll lie flat—then nail them right into the wall.

ANATOMY OF AN ORGANIZED GARDENING STATION

Outfit a rolling rack with easy-to-transport caddies and a mix of open and closed containers and you'll reap big rewards: The ability to inventory your supplies at a glance, instantly grab what you need—and save the digging for the flower beds.

1. A handy iron dispenser keeps twine from getting tangled and hangs from any hook.

2. Jute-lined bins conceal junky jumbles while preserving the overall orderly effect. Sweet zinc tags tied to the sides herald the contents.

3. Embrace change. Chalkboard end panels on rustic wooden cartons facilitate seasonal swaps.

4. The fix for wayward flowerpot saucers: a vintage dish drainer, which rarely costs more than a couple of bucks at flea markets.

5. Pull a bait and switch on the old tackle box. The fisherman's friend proves ideal for all those little odds and ends— twist ties, nails, etc.— that tend to get lost.

6. Borrow from the library. A secondhand card catalog doubles as a brilliant filing system for seed packets. (Any recipe box would fit the bill, too.)

7. A carpenter's caddy finds a new calling holding plant markers, stakes, and glass bottles filled with seeds or bird feed.

Call On Cubbies

Not everyone has the space for a fully stocked potting shed, with tools lined up in satisfying rows, scissors and twine always on hand, and a sink just for arranging flowers. But you can still bring order to your arsenal of outdoor essentials. Neatly gridded cabinets redefine dirty work without claiming much turf.

Left: This compact shelving unit expertly organizes petite possessions such as pots, seed packets, and flower frogs, and can fit atop a console table in a corner of the garage or mudroom.

Opposite: Towering columns of fruit crates nailed to a wall are roomy enough to harbor hardware (and horse-themed memorabilia) along with plant food and pots.

Climb the Walls

It's amazing what can happen when you give a familiar object a fresh backdrop. When displayed with a slew of similar shapes, even the most humdrum item becomes part of a larger-than-life collage.

Vintage pails and watering cans form a compelling composition against the weathered wood shingles of an exterior wall, and a 1900s oak work table laden with pots grounds the scene.

Garden tools read as graphic wall art against the grid of whitewashed planks and dark brown beams in this toolshed.

Extra sun hats and
beach totes warm up an
enclosed front porch,
which the homeowners
use as a second living
room in the summer
months.

HOMEWORK

Elevate garden tools with a DIY peg wall.

Oversized and awkwardly shaped tools can take up more than their fair share of storage space—unless you spread them across a spare wall with this genius peg rail adaptation.

1. Measure the wall's width and height and have three peg rails cut to fit: one with single pegs spaced evenly, one with pairs of pegs about four inches apart, and one with peg trios, also about four inches apart.

2. Make the double-peg rail the top one and use it to hang brooms, shovels, and rakes by their heads.

3. Halfway up the wall, install the single-peg rack, for small stuff like trowels, hats, and pruning shears.

4. Install the lowest rail—the one with three-peg clusters—just high enough to leave room for lidded bins of topsoil, compost, and mulch underneath, then wedge pairs of boots between its pegs.

TIP: You can also transplant this strategy to a utility closet or garage to get a grip on mops, brooms, buckets, stepladders, and more.

Photo Credits

Melanie Acevedo: 39

Lucas Allen: 6, 10-11, 23 top left, 25, 28, 34, 48 left, 59 top, 81, 101 left, 102, 129 top right, 136, 139, 145, 149, 151

Burcu Avsar: 67, 111 left, 112 left, 142

Quentin Bacon: 40 right, 121 left, 124 left

James Baigrie: 109 left

Christopher Baker: 148

Roland Bello: 17, 38 right

Aya Brackett: 58

Roger Davies/Trunk Archive: 143

Joseph De Leo: 79 top

Trevor Dixon: 132, 133

Tara Donne: 97 bottom right

Miki Duisterhof: 75, 83 right, 97 top right

Don Freeman: 13, 98

Dana Gallagher: 5 top, 12, 21 left, 27 left, 60 (both), 61, 70, 125, 146, 147 (both), 153

Tria Giovan: 135 top left

Alison Gootee/Studio D: 5 bottom, 21 right, 31, 50, 85 right, 106

Gridley + Graves: 23 bottom left, 36 right, 55, 126

John Gruen: 22, 141 bottom left

Alec Hemer: 44 right, 62, 68, 82, 109 right, 128, 131 top left, 144 left

Aimee Herring: 23 top right, 47 left, 57 right, 131 bottom left

Ray Kachatorian: 141 top right

Max Kim-Bee: 16 left, 24 left, 26, 29 bottom, 41, 44 left, 65, 76, 77 (all), 79 bottom, 89, 113, 114, 115, 118 left, 127 right, 130, 138

David A. Land: 131 top right

Kate Mathis: 94 left, 107, 111 right, 127 left

Ellen McDermott: 95

James Merrell: 38 left, 42 (both), 43, 46, 155

Keith Scott Morton: 27 right, 94 right, 112 right, 124 right, 135 top right, 135 bottom left

Laura Moss: 30, 71, 80 left, 83 left, 84, 86 (both), 87, 93 right, 120

Michael Partenio: 74 left, 104-105

Victoria Pearson: 15, 16 right, 18-19, 32, 47 right, 52, 56, 57 left, 63, 85 top left, 100, 101 right, 103, 108, 116

Nick Pope: 73 top, 80 right, 91

Steven Randazzo: 121 top right

Laura Resen: 118 right

Lara Robby/Studio D: 110, 121 bottom right

Lisa Romerein: 14, 20, 73 bottom, 93 left, 129 top left, 141 top left

Ellen Silverman: 51

Seth Smoot: 48 right, 90

Tim Street-Porter: 97 left, 150

Jonny Valiant: 78, 129 bottom left

Mikkel Vang: 24 right, 119

William Waldron: 152

Björn Wallander: 2, 8, 29 top, 35, 36 left, 40 left, 45, 49, 54, 59 bottom, 64, 66 left and right, 72, 74 right, 85 bottom left, 88, 96, 122, 123, 134, 140, 144 right

Wendell T. Webber: 92

Andrea Wyner: 37

FRONT COVER: Doug Steley C/Alamy

BACK COVER (from left): Max Kim-Bee, John Gruen, Lucas Allen

Index

Note: Page numbers in *italics* indicate photograph captions. Related photograph might be on opposite page.